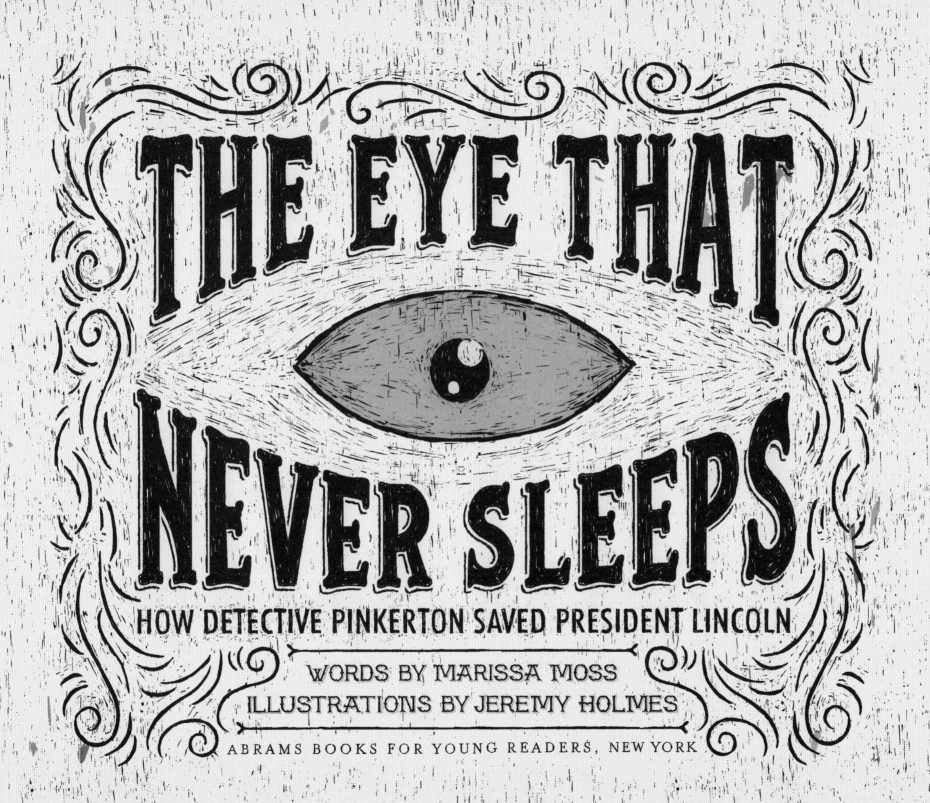

THE EYE THAT NEVER SLEEPS

HOW DETECTIVE PINKERTON SAVED PRESIDENT LINCOLN

WORDS BY MARISSA MOSS

ILLUSTRATIONS BY JEREMY HOLMES

ABRAMS BOOKS FOR YOUNG READERS, NEW YORK

WHAT DOES IT TAKE TO BE A GREAT DETECTIVE? Do You Need To Be STRONG OR RICH OR POWERFUL?

Allan Pinkerton wasn't any of those things. Born in 1819, he grew up in one of the worst slums in Scotland. But he had sharp eyes, a quick mind, and a hunger for justice. That passion for fairness led him to join a group promoting workers' rights. For years, the British government considered him a nuisance, then a criminal. When soldiers came to arrest him on his wedding day, Pinkerton fled with his bride, hiding on a ship that took them to America.

hey made their way to Chicago, where Pinkerton started a cooperage, a barrel business. In the 1840s practically everything was stored and shipped in barrels, from flour to apples and oil to wine. Pinkerton's shop was so successful that he soon had eight men working for him.

ALLAN PINKERTON'S COOPERAGE

One day in 1847, Pinkerton ran out of lumber, so he went to an island in a nearby river, a place where he often collected wood.

With his keen eyes, he noticed something more than wood, the remains of a campfire. Why would anybody camp out there? The island was isolated—not a natural place to stop while hunting or fishing or traveling.

inkerton was curious. He went back to the island night after night, waiting for the mysterious campers to return. On a dark night with only a sliver of moon in the sky, he discovered a ragtag group of men making something in a fire. Pinkerton couldn't see exactly what they were doing, only that the objects were small.

THERE COULD ONLY BE ONE
REASON

to make something late at night, hidden from everyone. Pinkerton shared his suspicions with the local sheriff. When the sheriff and his men went to the island the next night, Pinkerton came along. And that's how he helped capture a gang of counterfeiters, men making coins out of tin and lead.

When fake banknotes started appearing in a nearby town, the merchants asked Pinkerton to help. He'd caught the coin counterfeiters. Could he find the forgers of paper money, too? Pinkerton couldn't resist the challenge of solving the puzzle. He relied on the same skills he'd used so long ago in the slums—sharp eyes and a quick mind. And he caught the crooks!

The Chicago police were so impressed, they hired him as their first full-time detective. After a year on the force, Pinkerton decided to open his own agency.

inkerton relied on observation, logical deduction, and an understanding of people and their behavior. But he needed more than that to run an agency. He needed other agents with the same skills.

To teach these new detectives, Pinkerton wrote the *Pinkerton Method and Manual*:

1 How to shadow a suspect so he doesn't think you're following him.

2 How to disguise yourself and play a role (using the agency's large closet filled with clothes, wigs, and false mustaches).

3 How to engage suspects in conversation.

4 How to remember clues without taking notes a suspect might find later.

5 How to be determined and patient and observant.

CHAPTER

4

How to remember clues without taking notes a suspect might find later.

He also taught his agents to keep an open mind, to look for proof, and, most of all, to search for the truth. Justice above all!

His method worked so well that, by the 1850s, the Pinkerton Agency was the most successful detective agency in the country. Pinkerton solved more than 300 murders and recovered millions of dollars in stolen money. His sharp eye inspired the company logo with the slogan "We Never Sleep."

THE SOUTH ASSASSINATE LINCOLN · BALTIMORE · 8 · MEN PULL STRAWS · GETS OFF TRAIN

In 1860, Pinkerton was hired by the president of the Philadelphia, Wilmington, and Baltimore Railroad to protect the line from sabotage by secessionists, people advocating for the South to leave the Union. The rebels had warned they would blow up tracks around Washington, DC, cutting off the capital from supplies. Investigating these threats, Pinkerton heard disturbing rumors. A group in Baltimore was planning to ambush and kill Abraham Lincoln on his way to being sworn in as president.

WE'LL HAVE JUSTICE

LINCOLN MUST GO DURING THE DAY 8 MEN AND A PLAN

At first, Pinkerton thought the talk was just that, a lot of idle chatter. But he kept hearing troubling snippets from different sources, so Pinkerton sent agents to Baltimore, two men and one woman. Their job was to pose as secessionists, infiltrate the ring, and learn about the plot.

15

The news was even worse than Pinkerton feared. The plan included drawing lots to see which plotter would actually fire a deadly shot. The leaders worried that the chosen man might hesitate, so instead of one piece of red paper, they put in eight. Eight men would shoot at Lincoln as he rode through Baltimore on his way from one train depot to another. Once the deed was done, another group of conspirators would telegraph the news to their headquarters in Richmond, then cut all telegraph lines, destroy all bridges, and tear up all train tracks to keep word from traveling north.

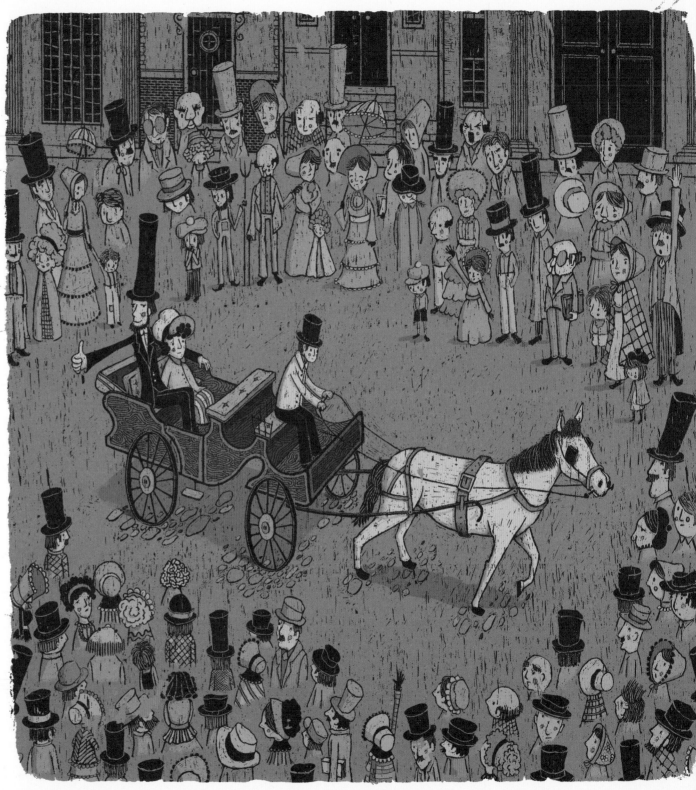

The Deed Is Done

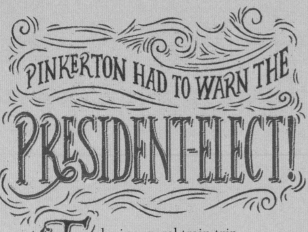

PINKERTON HAD TO WARN THE PRESIDENT-ELECT!

*T*he inaugural train trip from Springfield, Illinois, to Washington, DC, had been carefully organized to give as many Americans as possible the opportunity to see the new president and show their support in this tense, divisive time. The journey was meant to bring together a country on the verge of breaking apart over the heated issue of slavery.

Lincoln gave a speech at each whistle stop. Crowds lined the streets to see his carriage pass, and they surged into the hotels where he stayed. People followed him everywhere, even into private rooms. An aide was even hurt by the crushing mob. How could Pinkerton protect one man in such a throng?

Not trusting the mail or telegraph wires, Pinkerton sent an agent, Kate Warne, to set up an appointment so he could meet with Lincoln, then followed her to Philadelphia, the next city on the president's route. That night, he pushed his way through the excited crowds in the lobby and halls of the Continental Hotel. People were even gathered right outside Lincoln's door! This city was friendly to the president-elect. Here the hordes of people weren't a threat. What would it be like, though, with angry mobs in Baltimore, a city with strong southern sympathies?

To: Mr. Lincoln

Shall I send for Pinkerton?

YES!

KATE WARNE

UNDERCOVER

PHILADELPHIA

BALTIMORE

Pinkerton was let into the hotel room by Norman Judd, an Illinois state senator and close friend of Lincoln. The detective quickly outlined all the risks and how to avoid them. In his case notes, he wrote: "Mr. Lincoln was cool, calm, and collected . . . In fact, he did not appear to me to realize the great danger which was threatening him at that moment." Still, the president-elect agreed to Pinkerton's plan, so long as he didn't miss a single public event. The train had already zigged and zagged through Indianapolis, Columbus, Pittsburgh, Cleveland, Buffalo, Albany, New York, and Philadelphia. That still left Harrisburg and the last stop before DC: Baltimore.

The Deed   Is Done

incoln's route had been publicized in newspapers for weeks beforehand. Everyone knew he would arrive in Baltimore the morning of February 23. So the evening of the 22nd, the president's party—without the president—boarded the Harrisburg–Baltimore–DC train.

Lincoln would have a more convoluted route. He would take a special train back to Philadelphia from Harrisburg, then one directly to Baltimore from Philadelphia. The route was longer, but would get him to Baltimore earlier than the official presidential train. This was the trickiest part, as Lincoln would board the Baltimore-bound train in plain view of the other passengers and crew. So instead of his trademark stovepipe hat, he wore a soft hat and a shawl wrapped around his shoulders.

HARRISBURG

SECRET ROUTE

PHILADELPHIA

ORIGINAL ROUTE

BALTIMORE

WASHINGTON

MAP OF PINKERTON'S PLAN

Kate Warne, the Pinkerton agent, was waiting for the president in the sleeping car of the Philadelphia-to-Baltimore train (not the special presidential one that had already left with Mrs. Lincoln). She'd told the conductor she needed the secluded rear berths for herself and her invalid brother. In her detective report, Warne noted, "Mr. Lincoln is very homely, and so very tall that he could not lay straight on his berth . . . The excitement seemed to keep us all awake. Nothing of importance happened through the night."

Meanwhile, as an extra precaution to be sure that the conspirators couldn't warn anyone of a change in travel plans, Pinkerton had the telegraph wires "fixed" so that any dispatches between Harrisburg and Baltimore would be intercepted and delivered straight to Pinkerton himself.

But what if Lincoln's train missed the transfer in Philadelphia? Pinkerton couldn't take the chance that the Baltimore-bound train would leave without the president. So he asked the railroad superintendent to instruct the conductor that the train couldn't leave until an important package arrived.

The wrapped parcel, looking very official, arrived shortly after Lincoln did and was given to the conductor along with permission to leave. What was in the important package? A newspaper. Just something to be sure the train waited for its most important passenger, the real package.

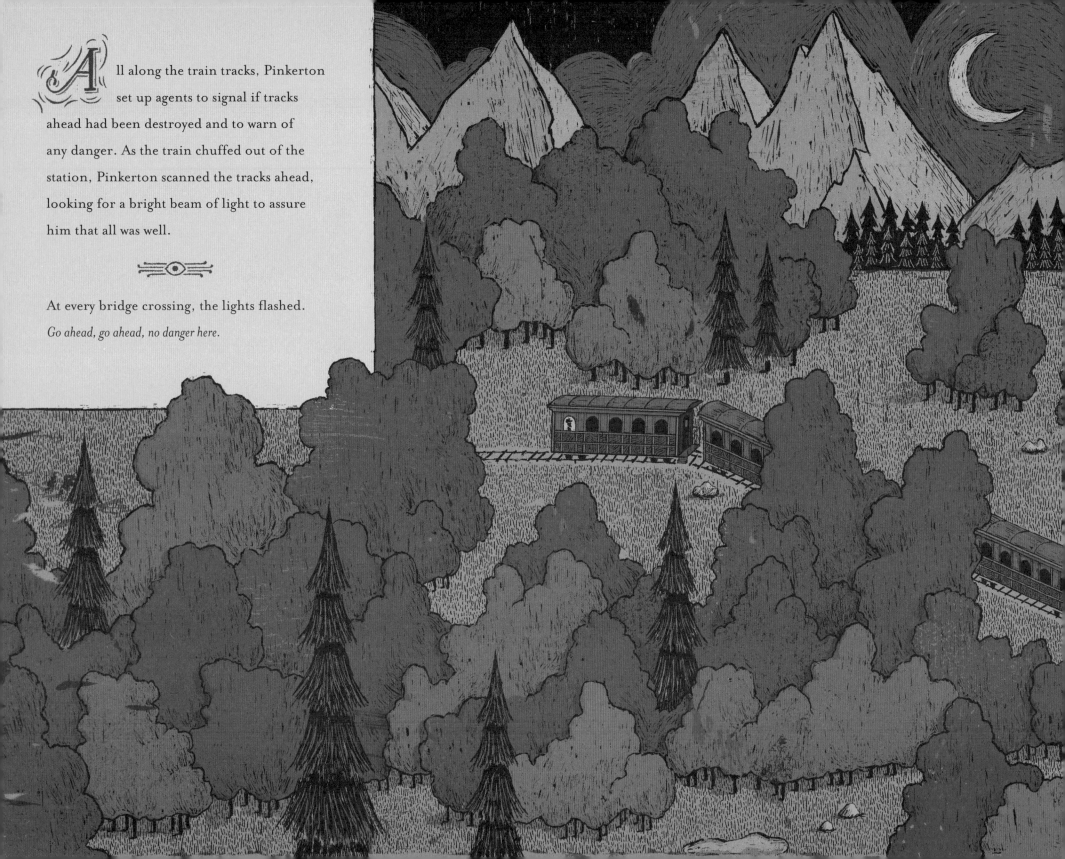

All along the train tracks, Pinkerton set up agents to signal if tracks ahead had been destroyed and to warn of any danger. As the train chuffed out of the station, Pinkerton scanned the tracks ahead, looking for a bright beam of light to assure him that all was well.

At every bridge crossing, the lights flashed.
Go ahead, go ahead, no danger here.

The train reached Baltimore in darkness, at 3:30 a.m. Instead of the planned presidential parade in full light of day through the streets from one train depot to the other, the sleeping car was quietly detached from the Philadelphia train and drawn by horses along the streets to the Camden Street Station.

The streets were still, the silence broken only by the sounds of the horses' hooves. The conspirators were all asleep in their beds, waiting for morning to attack Lincoln.

nce at the station, the train was due to leave right away for DC. Fifteen minutes went by, then an hour, and still the train didn't leave. Two tense hours passed with the sleeping car stuck in the station. Nobody was sleeping, Pinkerton least of all. Lincoln joked quietly that the city of Baltimore loved him more than Pinkerton thought, since it was keeping him there so long.

Finally, the train started moving. It had been waiting for late-arriving cargo from the West. Pinkerton didn't relax until after arriving in DC shortly before dawn.

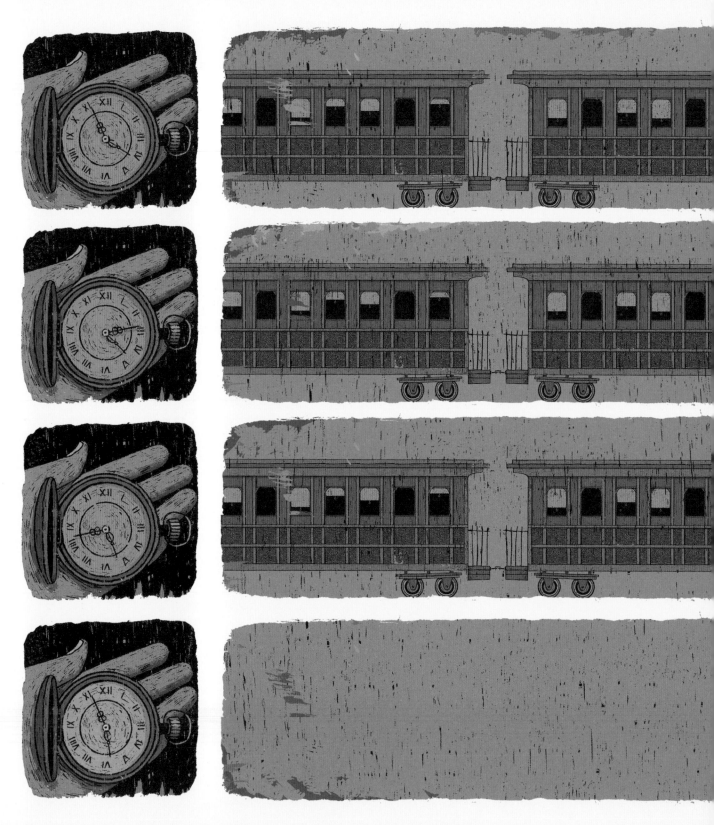

BALTIMORE

AFTER SAFELY DELIVERING THE

PRESIDENT-ELECT,

Pinkerton sent a coded telegram to his partner
at the detective agency back in Chicago:
PLUMS HAS NUTS—ARRI'D AT BARLEY—ALL RIGHT.
E. J. ALLEN

E. J. Allen was the fake name Pinkerton always
used while undercover. "Plums" was code for
Pinkerton; "Barley" was code for DC. You can
guess who "Nuts" was code for.

THE MORSE TELEGRAPH ALPHABET

A . —
B — . . .
C . . .
D — . .
E .
F . — .
G — — .
H . . . .
I . .
J — . — .
K — . —
L —
M — —
N — .
O . .
P . . . . .
Q . . — .
R . . .
S . . .
T —
U . . —
V . . . —
W . — —
X . — . .
Y . . . .
Z . . . .
& . . . .

WASHINGTON

When the conspirators heard their plot had failed, they fled Baltimore, heading south to fight for the Confederacy.

41

One of Lincoln's first acts as president was to create the Secret Service to spy on the Confederacy and catch southern spies, many of whom were working in DC. He knew just the man to lead this top security group: Allan Pinkerton.

The boy who had grown up in a slum was now working for the president of the United States, using those skills he'd developed long ago—sharp eyes, a keen mind, and a passion for justice.

His agency still exists today. The Eye Never Sleeps!

TIME LINE

August 25, 1819: Allan Pinkerton born in Glasgow, Scotland

1829: Pinkerton's father dies; Allan Pinkerton drops out of school to work to support his family

1834–1842: Active in British Chartist movement, advocating workers' rights

March 1842: Married Joan Carfrae in Glasgow (or U.S.—sources conflict on this)

1842: Emigrated to United States

August 4, 1843: Daughter Isabelle McQueen Pinkerton born (died May 23, 1863)

The Pinkerton Agency logo gave rise to the term "private eye" as a nickname for detectives.

1844: Pinkerton's home becomes a stop on the Underground Railway, helping enslaved people north to freedom

April 7, 1846: Son William Pinkerton born (died December 11, 1923)

1847: Discovers ring of counterfeiters

December 2, 1848: Twins born, Robert (died August 12, 1907) and Joan (died March 4, 1855)

1849: Appointed first detective in Chicago Police force

1850: Started North-Western Police Agency, soon to be called Pinkerton & Co., then Pinkerton National Detective Agency. His logo of an eye, along with the slogan "We Never Sleep" became the inspiration for the term "private eye."

June 13, 1852: Daughter Mary born (died July 17, 1854)

July 22, 1855: Daughter Joan born (died January 25, 1940)

1856: Hired Kate Warne, first woman detective in United States

1859: Attended secret abolitionist meetings with John Brown, Frederick Douglass, John Jones, and Henry Wagoner

November 1860: Abraham Lincoln elected 16th president

Allan Pinkerton (*left*), President Lincoln, and Maj. Gen. John A. McClernand at the Battle of Antietam, 1862. Photographer Alexander Gardner, courtesy of the Library of Congress.

November 1860: Hired by Philadelphia, Wilmington, and Baltimore Railroad for security, to protect the line from sabotage

December–February 1861: Thwarts planned assassination plot against president-elect Lincoln

March 1861: Lincoln inaugurated as president

April 1861–May 1865: Headed intelligence service for new administration, an organization created to spy on the southern confederacy and discover their spies in the Union, especially in DC

April 15, 1865: Lincoln assassinated in Washington, DC

1870s: Successfully infiltrated and caught Butch Cassidy and his Wild Bunch, but failed to arrest bank robbers Jesse and Frank James

1850s–1880s: Compiled first "database" of criminals, a collection of files with photographs and descriptions of criminals

July 1, 1884: Died in Chicago

July 1884: The agency was taken over by Pinkerton's two sons, William and Robert. They closed the women's division and took the agency in a direction not foreseen by their father. Industrialists hired the agency to spy on unions or act as guards. Pinkerton agents violently fought with strikers during the Homestead Mill Strike in 1892, using bricks, guns, and even dynamite as weapons. Seven agents and nine strikers died in the melee. The agency was involved in so many aggressive labor disputes through the early twentieth century that the company was called the "Pinks."

1893: The Anti-Pinkerton act is passed, making it illegal for the agency to take on the kind of work it has since 1871, investigating federal crimes. The FBI now does this work.

1937: The agency moves away from strikebreaking activities, turning instead to security and protection services. Detectives are no longer even hired after 1960.

July 2003: William J. Burns Detective Agency acquires the Pinkerton Agency, then acquired by Securitas AB, currently called Securitas Security Services USA, one of the largest protection services and security company in the world.

ARTIST'S NOTE

The Eye That Never Sleeps is the first nonfiction book I have illustrated. My favorite part of preparing the illustrations was the research required—from the mastheads of period newspapers to Lincoln's famed hat, I wanted to represent everything in its proper historical context. I read books like Samantha Seiple's *Lincoln's Spymaster* and the Smithsonian's *Train: The Definitive Visual History*. I turned to vintagefashionguild.org for the fashions of the time and scoured other websites to find old newspapers and hand-drawn antique maps as well as architecture and other period objects. The mid-1800s is hands down my favorite era for typography: The board games of the McLaughlin Brothers are a great source!

I create a specific look for every book I do. For this project, I had planned to create a period piece with woodcut, scratchboard, or etching, using color to make it contemporary. Looking at the large pile of sketches, I realized that woodcuts would be a very ambitious undertaking. Scratchboard? It has a similar look and feel to woodcut. Unable to find boards big enough, I handmade two, which took an entire day. After about an hour of scratching away, I realized the scratchboard process wasn't feasible timewise, either. What to do? I spent a Saturday developing a digital scratchboard style. It's not that different from traditional scratchboarding. There is a black screen. You don't draw the black lines; you create the space around the black lines. You draw the negative space. What made the process doable was that there was no prep work . . . no boardmaking . . . no transfer of the sketch onto the board. With the digital approach, you place your sketch under the black layer, but it is still visible. Scratching away the art is time-consuming, but the setup is instant. Don't get me wrong—I was nervous. But two spreads in, I fell in love with how things were looking and decided to take the gamble. I'm glad I did!

AUTHOR'S NOTE

Born in Glasgow, Scotland, Allan Pinkerton (1819–1884) started working when he was ten in one of the textile factories that hired children for their small, nimble fingers. He was mostly self-educated and loved to read. As a teenager, he became one of the youngest leaders in the Chartist movement, a group promoting workers' rights and votes for all men at a time when only those with enough property could vote. The group was considered criminal by the British government. When Pinkerton saw other members arrested and thrown into jail, he decided to leave his homeland for North America.

In fact, soldiers were coming to arrest him on his wedding day, so instead of going to the altar, he and his bride, Joan Carfrae, fled, getting married as soon as they could (they later had two sons and four daughters). In 1849, Pinkerton was appointed the first detective in Chicago. A year later, he set up the North-Western Police Agency with a lawyer for a partner, Edward Rucker. This became Pinkerton & Co. and then Pinkerton National Detective Agency. The secret service he founded under President Lincoln was the forerunner of the U.S. Secret Service. His work with spies became the basis for the CIA.

In October 1856, Pinkerton hired Kate Warne as the first woman detective in the United States. She was so good, he hired others (fifty years before any police department in America) and put Kate in charge of all the female agents, as well as managing the DC office during the Civil War.

While Pinkerton insisted that detectives must combine "considerable intellectual power and knowledge of human nature," he discouraged them from coercing confessions or taking statements from witnesses who were drunk. Above everything else, he valued the truth. He insisted that his detectives keep an open mind. His manual directed: "The object of every investigation . . . is to come at the whole truth . . . There must be no endeavoring, therefore, to over-color or exaggerate anything against any particular individual, whatever the suspicion may be against him."

Pinkerton honored the law but held himself to an even higher moral standard. Despite the Fugitive Slave Act of 1850, Pinkerton's Chicago home was one of the stops on the Underground Railroad. His house was often filled with runaways and their guides, including John Brown. Pinkerton and his wife provided clean clothes, hot food, and a place to rest for all of them. In March 1859, Brown hinted to Pinkerton about his plans for armed insurrection during his last stay at the house. As Brown left, Pinkerton turned to his sons and said, "Look well upon that man. He is greater than Napoleon and just as great as George Washington."

Pinkerton ran the intelligence agency for President Lincoln during the Civil War the same way he'd run his detective agency. He honed the art of "spycraft" and excelled in choosing agents who were incorruptible. One of his best agents, Timothy Webster, was part of the team that foiled the Baltimore assassination plot, and he became a very successful spy. Webster was so convincing as a supporter of the South that Confederate officers trusted him with important documents and information, all of which he passed on to Pinkerton.

When embarrassed officials in Richmond learned his real identity, he was hanged, the first spy to be executed during the Civil War. The soldier who was recruited to replace him was Frank Thompson, really Sarah Emma Edmonds, a woman disguised as a man, whose story you can read in *Nurse, Soldier, Spy* (a picture book) and *A Soldier's Secret* (a young adult novel).

After the Civil War, Pinkerton went on to chase after some of the most famous desperadoes of the Wild West, including Jesse James, the Dalton gang, and Butch Cassidy and the Wild Bunch.

Ironically, considering his prounion roots, Pinkerton's sons, who ran the company after their father's death, accepted cases working for industrialists to provide information on union-organizing efforts. While Pinkerton had always insisted that workers be treated with respect and that his agents only use violence in self-defense, the agency became synonymous with union-bashing after the high-profile Chicago Haymarket Riot of 1886 and the Pennsylvania Homestead Strike of 1892, incidents that both involved Pinkerton agents.

At the time of Pinkerton's death in 1884, he was working on a system to keep records of criminals, a tool now used in digital form by the FBI. Pinkerton's agency, despite the mistakes made by his sons, including the closing of the women's department, continued to thrive, opening offices throughout the world. In 1999, the Pinkerton Agency was acquired by Securitas Security Services USA, Inc, the biggest private security agency in the world. All over the globe, the Eye Never Sleeps!

ENDNOTES

22   "Mr. Lincoln was cool, calm, and collected . . ." Allan Pinkerton, *History and evidence of the passage of Abraham Lincoln . . . from Harrisburg, Pa., to Washington, D.C.*, on the 22nd and 23rd of February, 1861, Chicago, Republican Print, 1868, 19.

28   "Mr. Lincoln is very homely . . ." Norma Cuthbert, ed., *Lincoln and the Baltimore Plot, 1861, From Pinkerton Reports and Related Papers*, 69

38   "Plums has nuts . . ." Ibid., 84.

40   "We are not enemies but friends." Abraham Lincoln, "The Inaugural Address of the President of the United States, on The Fourth of March, 1861." *Chicago Tribune*. March 4, 1861.

46   The account of John Brown's visit to Chicago is drawn from the *Chicago Times*, September 1, 1882; and Allan Pinkerton, *The Spy of the Rebellion*, xxvi, 36, 233–34.

BIBLIOGRAPHY

Cuthbert, Norma, ed. *Lincoln and the Baltimore Plot, 1861, From Pinkerton Reports and Related Papers*. Huntington Library, San Marino, CA: 1949.

Harnett, Kane. *Spies for the Blue and Gray*. Garden City, NY: Hanover House, 1954.

Horan, James D. *The Pinkertons: The Detective Dynasty that Made History*. New York: Crown Publishers, 1967.

Horan, James, and Howard Swiggett. *The Pinkerton Story*. New York: Putnam, 1951.

Jeffreys-Jones, Rhodri. *Cloak and Dollar: A History of American Secret Intelligence*. New Haven, CT: Yale University Press, 2003.

Lincoln, Abraham. "The Inaugural Address of the President of the United States, on The Fourth of March, 1861." *Chicago Tribune*. March 4, 1861. From the Gilder Lehrman Institute of American History.

Mackay, James. *Allan Pinkerton: The First Private Eye*. New York: John Wiley & Sons, 1996.

Markle, Donald. *Spies and Spymasters of the Civil War*. New York: Hippocrene Books, 1994.

Mason, John Potter. *Thirteen Desperate Days*. New York: Ivan Obolensky, 1964.

Morn, Frank. *The Eye That Never Sleeps: a History of the Pinkerton National Detective Agency*. Bloomington, IN: Indiana University Press, 1982.

Pinkerton, Allan. *The Expressman and the Detective*. New York: Arno Press, 1976.

——. *History and Evidence of the Passage of Abraham Lincoln from Harrisburg, PA, to Washington, D.C. on the 22nd and 23rd of February, 1861*. Chicago: Pinkerton National Detective Agency, 1907.

——. *Mississippi Outlaws and the Detectives*. New York: G.W. Carleton., 1889.

——. *Thirty Years a Detective*. New York: G. W. Carleton., 1884.

Potter, John Mason. *Thirteen Desperate Days*. New York: Ivan Obolensky, 1964.

Rowan, Richard Wilmer. *The Pinkertons: A Detective Dynasty*. Boston: Little, Brown, 1931.

Stashower, Daniel. *The Hour of Peril: The Secret Plot to Murder Lincoln Before the Civil War*. New York: Minotaur Books, 2013.

Voss, Frederick, and James Barber. *We Never Sleep: The First Fifty Years of the Pinkertons*. Washington, DC: Smithsonian Institution Press, 1981.

Wilson, Douglas, and Rodney Davis, eds. *Herndon's Informants: Letters, Interviews, and Statements*. Chicago: University of Illinois Press, 1998.

INDEX

This story was inspired by my great-uncle Sam, himself a Pinkerton detective. Like many of the agents Pinkerton hired, Sam was an immigrant with a thick accent, and not many people would give him a job. That hadn't stopped Pinkerton, himself an immigrant.
—M.M.

For Jennifer—without your encouragement and support, none of this would have been possible.
—J.H.

The art in this book is digitally rendered and colored scratchboard.

Cataloging-in-Publication Data has been applied for and may be obtained from the Library of Congress.

ISBN 978-1-4197-3064-1

Text copyright © 2018 Marissa Moss
Illustrations copyright © 2018 Jeremy Holmes
Book design by Jeremy Holmes and Julia Marvel

Published in 2018 by Abrams Books for Young Readers, an imprint of ABRAMS.

Printed and bound in China
10 9 8 7 6 5 4 3 2 1

Abrams Books for Young Readers are available at special discounts when purchased in quantity for premiums and promotions as well as fundraising or educational use. Special editions can also be created to specification. For details, contact specialsales@abramsbooks.com or the address below.

ABRAMS The Art of Books
195 Broadway, New York, NY 10007
abramsbooks.com